Lucie Papineau • Caroline Hamel

THE STRONGEST MAN IN THE WORLD

THE LEGEND OF LOUIS CYR

AUZOU

There once was a little boy named Cyprien-Noé Cyr. The eldest of seventeen children, he was born in 1863 to a poor family in a small village in Quebec. Although he was a robust child, no one imagined he would become the legendary Louis Cyr, the strongest man in the world!

No one that is, except his grandfather, Pierre. Grandpa Pierre had spent his life running, trapping, and hunting. He was a legend in the region. Grandpa loved Cyprien-Noé, and Cyprien-Noé adored his grandpa. He took the boy with him wherever he went.

His grandson's favorite place to go was the blacksmith shop where Mr. Trudeau reigned supreme. The young boy never tired of watching him hammer the red-hot horseshoes into shape. He watched in wonder as the master blacksmith lifted the heavy anvil as if it were a feather! "Someday, I'll be strong," said Cyprien-Noé, "just like Grandpa and Mr. Trudeau."

The boy surprised everyone in the village with his first display of strength when he was just eight years old.

His father asked him to find a young calf that had wandered off. He found the lost animal, but the calf was stuck in some mud. He pulled the calf loose, but the animal was too tired and couldn't stand up. So, Cyprien-Noé picked up the calf, draped him across his shoulders, and carried him all the way home.

Cyprien-Noé was a hero!

The following year, Cyprien-Noé began attending the village school. Because attendance was not mandatory in Quebec, he left after only three years. He couldn't read or write very well, but he *was* the schoolyard champion at wrestling, throwing sticks, and lifting everything he saw!

His family was poor, and there were many of mouths to feed, so he left school at twelve and began looking for work. Although he was quite muscular, his chubby face and curly hair made him look too young to be capable of hard work.

This changed the day Cyprien-Noé went walking in the woods where he discovered Irénée Gagnon, who ran a logging camp. Lost, Mr. Gagnon had sprained his ankle and couldn't walk back to his horse and cart. Rather than running to the village for help, the boy picked him up and carried him on his shoulders to his cart. The man was so impressed that he immediately hired him.

Life wasn't easy for lumberjacks in 1875. There were no machines or chain saws. They had only their strength, axes, and saws to fell the trees. Young Cyr surprised everyone. He carried tools, drove teams of horses, and broke off the branches of large trees by himself. He worked harder than men twice his age!

Cyprien-Noé was almost fifteen when his family decided to move to the United States. The family had gotten larger with each passing year. Their income from farming and work in the lumber camp was no longer enough to feed eleven hungry mouths.

The family gathered their meager possessions and squeezed aboard a train.
Three days later, they arrived in Lowell, a small industrial town near Boston.

It was common at that time for workers to take new, easier to pronounce names when first entering the US. Cyprien-Noé's parents changed his to Louis. His father hoped to find work in one of the local textile mills, but he was counting on his son to help. Louis did not disappoint. Easily lifting 180-pound boxes of cotton, he was soon earning the wages of two men.

Louis Cyr's reputation as the Canadian Samson spread like wildfire. Strong men came from all around to compete with him, and every time, the young factory worker from Quebec won.
Louis could lift boulders, free mired carts, and beat the strongest men at arm wrestling.

But it wasn't until he met his first coach, Professor Donovan,
that he learned the professional sport of weight lifting.

Young Louis not only learned to lift weights, but how to play the violin! He loved to play tunes and could dance a mean jig, a surprising feat for someone his size.
One night at a dance, fate stepped in, and Louis met a lovely, petite girl named Melina.
It was love at first sight! To him, she was the belle of the ball.
Barely eighteen when they met, they married less than a year later.

The couple returned to Quebec where Louis prepared to challenge a new opponent: David Michaud, the reigning king of Canadian strongmen. They would take turns lifting heavy stones. The first weighed 45 pounds, the last, more than 507 pounds. A large crowd came from far and wide to watch the show. They were awestruck when Louis succeeded in lifting every stone, including the heaviest one! This was something no one else had ever accomplished, and they named Louis the new strongest man in Canada.

The news quickly spread. Everyone wanted to see the incredible Louis Cyr in action, so Louis and Melina joined the circus and took to the road. One of his most popular performances was when he played tug-of-war with four draft horses at the same time. He was so powerful that the horses couldn't move him an inch!

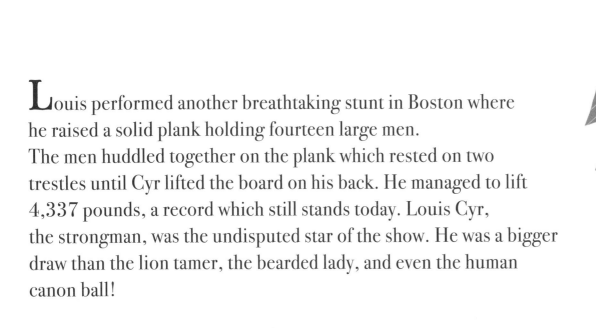

Louis performed another breathtaking stunt in Boston where
he raised a solid plank holding fourteen large men.
The men huddled together on the plank which rested on two
trestles until Cyr lifted the board on his back. He managed to lift
4,337 pounds, a record which still stands today. Louis Cyr,
the strongman, was the undisputed star of the show. He was a bigger
draw than the lion tamer, the bearded lady, and even the human
canon ball!

But what was the source of his incredible strength? Was it his long Samson-like hair? No. Louis believed, as did others at the time, that it came from what he ate. Every day he ate almost nine pounds of meat, six or seven bowls of soup, as well as bread, potatoes, and washed it all down with gallons of milk. Some say he once ate an entire roast piglet in a single meal!
Louis Cyr certainly set some unusual records.

By now, Louis was the champion of North America, and his reputation had spread to Europe. The time had come for him to cross the Atlantic to face their strongest men.

But no one dared take up the challenge, despite his open invitation. They knew they could never beat a man with records so incredible that they defied comprehension.

When Louis returned from Europe undefeated, he brought with him the title: Strongest Man in the World!

The world-famous Louis Cyr—the poor boy from the village of Saint-Cyprien—had fulfilled his dream, and that of his grandpa. Admired by his friends and family, he was looked up to by many of the French Canadians working as farmers and lumberjacks, or in the factories of New England.

At last he could enjoy a quiet, peaceful life with his wife and their daughter, Emiliana... the two suns in his universe.

The End